STAR WARS

JEDI HEROES

INTRODUCTION

The Jedi Order uphold peace and justice across the LEGO® *Star Wars* galaxy. Learn all about these powerful beings—from the wise Grand Master Yoda to the brave Ahsoka Tano.

Introduction
MEET THE MINIFIGURES

HOW TO USE THIS BOOK

These amazing minifigures are ordered according to the *Star Wars*® property in which they first appeared or mostly featured. Tabs at the top of each page indicate which properties this minifgure appears in. As most Star Wars characters appear in the Expanded Universe, that tab is highlighted only if a minifigure appears in an EU set. The Clone Wars tab has not been highlighted if the character has a separate Clone Wars minifigure.

This book also includes variants of featured minifigures, which are the same character, but have some modifications that make them different in some way.

Contents

EPISODE I

Qui-Gon Jinn **6**
Obi-Wan Kenobi (Padawan) **7**
Yoda **8**
Mace Windu **9**

EPISODE II

Obi-Wan Kenobi (Jedi Knight) **10**
Anakin Skywalker (Padawan) **11**

CLONE WARS

Ahsoka Tano **12**
Yoda (CW) **13**
Anakin Skywalker (CW) **14**
Luminara Unduli (CW) **15**
Plo Koon **16**
Nahdar Vebb **17**
Mace Windu (CW) **18**
Obi-Wan Kenobi (CW) **19**
Eeth Koth **20**
Aayla Secura **21**
Shaak Ti **22**
Ki-Adi-Mundi **23**
Saesee Tiin **24**
Quinlan Vos **25**

EPISODE III

Obi-Wan Kenobi (Jedi Master) **26**
Kit Fisto **27**
Anakin Skywalker (Jedi Knight) **28**
Barriss Offee **29**

Acknowledgments **30**

Maverick Jedi Master Qui-Gon Jinn has appeared in seven LEGO *Star Wars* sets since 1999. There are four slightly different variants of Qui-Gon, but he always appears in his Jedi robe and tunic, ready to undertake a mission for the Jedi Order. Each variant has either his unique brown hair or a brown hood, which helps him to keep a low profile.

STAR VARIANT

Qui-Gon wrong
In the Republic Cruiser (set 7665), Qui-Gon has tan legs, a hood... and the wrong head! His head is Obi-Wan Kenobi's from General Grievous Chase (set 7255). It was later replaced with the correct head.

Qui-Gon's cut
Qui-Gon's long, pulled-back hairstyle has only ever been used on his minifigure. It first appeared on his original variant (in various sets from 1999–2000) and has since been resurrected for his 2011 redesign.

Jedi robes are a standard brown fabric cape

Green lightsaber blade with silver hilt

Updated Jedi tunic and utility belt design is new for 2011

Qui-Gon Jinn
JEDI MASTER

DATA FILE
SET: 7961 Darth Maul's Sith Infiltrator
YEAR: 2011
PIECES: 5
EQUIPMENT: Cape, hood, lightsaber
VARIANTS: 4

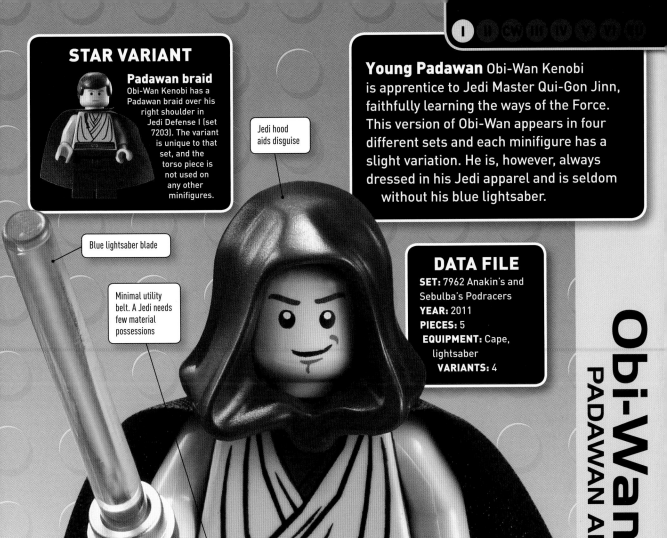

STAR VARIANT

Padawan braid
Obi-Wan Kenobi has a Padawan braid over his right shoulder in Jedi Defense I (set 7203). The variant is unique to that set, and the torso piece is not used on any other minifigures.

Jedi hood aids disguise

Young Padawan Obi-Wan Kenobi is apprentice to Jedi Master Qui-Gon Jinn, faithfully learning the ways of the Force. This version of Obi-Wan appears in four different sets and each minifigure has a slight variation. He is, however, always dressed in his Jedi apparel and is seldom without his blue lightsaber.

Blue lightsaber blade

Minimal utility belt. A Jedi needs few material possessions

DATA FILE
SET: 7962 Anakin's and Sebulba's Podracers
YEAR: 2011
PIECES: 5
EQUIPMENT: Cape, lightsaber
VARIANTS: 4

Obi-Wan Kenobi
PADAWAN APPRENTICE

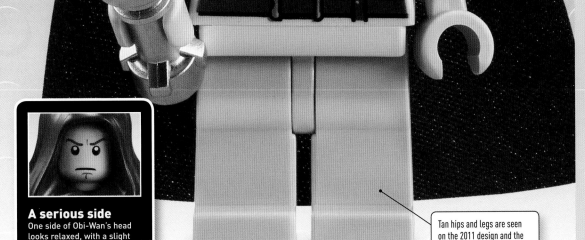

A serious side
One side of Obi-Wan's head looks relaxed, with a slight smile, but the other is more serious and ready for action.

Tan hips and legs are seen on the 2011 design and the variant found in the Republic Cruiser (set 7665)

7

Wise Jedi Master Mace Windu appears in brown Jedi robes and a blue-gray tunic in Clone Turbo Tank (set 7261). He is the only minifigure to wield a purple lightsaber, and in the 2005 release of the set, its powerful blade lights up to make it look even more impressive. A similar Mace with a non-light-up lightsaber appears in the 2006 reissue of the set.

Clone Turbo Tank (set 7261)
Mace Windu takes part in the Battle of Kashyyyk in Clone Turbo Tank. In the 2006 reissue of the set, Mace brandishes a normal lightsaber and has removeable parts.

Purple lightsaber blade is removeable from the hilt

Head button operates light-up lightsaber

Mace Windu
LEGENDARY JEDI MASTER

DATA FILE
SET: 7261 Clone Turbo Tank
YEAR: 2005/6
PIECES: 1
EQUIPMENT: Cape, lightsaber
VARIANTS: 2

Mace has no right hand piece—his right arm extends into the lightsaber hilt

Light-up lightsaber
The head, torso, hips, right arm, and lightsaber hilt are not removeable on Light-up Lightsaber minifigures. This allows electric current to flow from a battery in the torso to an LED in the lightsaber hilt when the head button is pressed.

Reddish-brown cloth cape can't be removed

An old Jedi

Yoda is over 900 years old! Although he can leap through the air during a lightsaber duel like a Jedi half his age, his minifigure also comes with a wooden walking stick in X-Wing Fighter (set 4502).

As Grand Master of the Jedi Order, Yoda is the most respected Jedi in the LEGO *Star Wars* galaxy—despite his small size. Although Yoda's minifigure is dressed in the traditional tan robes of a Jedi, he is easily recognizable by his short legs, unique head sculpt, and green skin color.

DATA FILE

SET: 7103 Jedi Duel
YEAR: 2002
PIECES: 3
EQUIPMENT: Lightsaber
VARIANTS: 1

Yoda's head is made of rubber instead of the ABS plastic used for most LEGO pieces

Getting a head

Yoda's unique sand-green head with large, distinctive ears was designed specifically for his 2002 minifigure. It is a different mold from the Clone Wars version of Yoda (p.13), which was first released in 2009.

Yoda's tan and brown torso looks similar to those of other Jedi, but the patterns are unique to him

Yoda's species has never been revealed

Yoda is smaller than most other Jedi, but his lightsaber is standard LEGO size

Yoda
JEDI GRAND MASTER

Front and back

Yoda is always on guard: His back is never turned. But his utility belt and Jedi robes pattern are printed on the back of his torso, too.

Yoda was the first LEGO minifigure to have short, unposeable legs

As a skilled Jedi Knight, Obi-Wan Kenobi is focused and controlled at a time of turmoil in the LEGO *Star Wars* galaxy. Two variants of his minifigure have starred in two sets; in both he faces dangerous challenges that require great judgment. He pursues bounty hunter Jango Fett in Jedi Starfighter (set 7143), and Zam Wesell in Bounty Hunter Pursuit (set 7133).

Jedi Starfighter (set 7143)
Jedi Master Obi-Wan Kenobi pilots a Delta-7 starfighter in this 2002 set—the only one to feature the Obi-Wan variant with a headset. The minifigure has binoculars and a lightsaber, but he has nowhere to store them when he zooms into flight mode.

Obi-Wan Kenobi
JEDI KNIGHT

DATA FILE
SET: 7143 Jedi Starfighter
YEAR: 2002
PIECES: 4
EQUIPMENT: Lightsaber, electrobinoculars
VARIANTS: 2

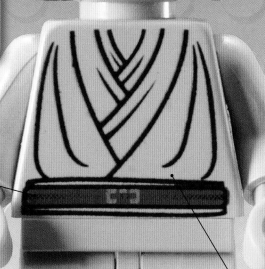

Most Jedi Knights wear their hair long

This minifigure has a neatly trimmed beard and wears a headset on his head. The variant in Bounty Hunter Pursuit (set 7133), is identical but without the headset

Utility belt for Jedi essentials

Obi-Wan shares his Jedi tunic torso with two minifigures: his old mentor Qui-Gon Jinn (p.6) and the young Padawn version of himself (p.7)

Knight flight
Obi-Wan Kenobi's long Jedi Knight hair is standard female LEGO hair. The hair piece in Obi-Wan's dark orange color is worn by only one other minifigure: a female airline passenger in the LEGO World City theme.

Headstrong Padawan Anakin Skywalker is training under his more cautious mentor Obi-Wan Kenobi. The minifigure has broken away from Jedi tradition by wearing a torso piece with dark Jedi robes—this coupled with Anakin's half smiling face could suggest a darkness within him that he cannot control.

Bounty Hunter Pursuit (set 7133)
The Padawan Anakin minifigure is involved in a fast-paced pursuit in this 2002 set, which is the only one to feature this version of Anakin. He and Obi-Wan Kenobi are chasing changeling assassin Zam Wesell on Coruscant. The Jedi minifigures can store their lightsabers within a secret compartment in their airspeeder.

As is befitting of a unique Jedi like Anakin, his slight smile was designed specifically for his Padawan minifigure

Earth orange
Anakin's earth orange hair-color is unusual for a LEGO minifigure. Only three others have it: Uncle Vernon Dursley (who has the same hair piece as Anakin), and Ron and Ginny Weasley, all from the LEGO Harry Potter theme.

Padawan learner braid

Padawan Anakin wears a Jedi tunic with a protective black surcoat. His torso piece is unique to him

A variant of this minifigure appears in Tusken Raider Encounter (set 7113) and has a brown cape

Anakin Skywalker
JEDI PADAWAN

DATA FILE
SET: 7133 Bounty Hunter Pursuit
YEAR: 2002
PIECES: 4
EQUIPMENT: Lightsaber
VARIANTS: 2

Ahsoka Tano
EAGER PADAWAN

Ahsoka Tano is Anakin Skywalker's enthusiastic Padawan. She has fought for the Republic in six Clone Wars sets since her 2008 release. As a Togruta, Ahsoka's minifigure has brightly colored skin and striped head-tails. She wears an unusual Jedi costume, including a brown top and matching gloves.

Unique head piece features Ahsoka's orange skin and white face markings

LEGO Togrutas
For a while, Ahsoka was the only Togruta character available in minifigure form. In 2011, however, Jedi Master Shaak Ti's red-skinned minifigure was released, with fully grown, adult-length head-tails (see p.22).

Head-tails
Ahsoka's hair piece is not hair at all! It is a unique mold of the blue and white head-tails that grow from the heads of all Togrutas.

Ahsoka's head-tails aren't yet full-length because she is still young

Unique torso is printed with Ahsoka's orange skin and distinctive Jedi costume. There is no printing on the back

Utility belt with storage pouch and food capsules

Until 2009, Ahsoka's lightsaber hilt was a matte gray color

DATA FILE
SET: 8098 Clone Turbo Tank
YEAR: 2010
PIECES: 4
EQUIPMENT: Lightsaber
VARIANTS: 1

Boba Fett is the only other minifigure to have the same brown hip piece and light-gray legs combination

Armored Assault Tank (set 8018)

Clone Wars Yoda only appears in this one set, where he and a single clone trooper take on two battle droids, three super battle droids, and an armored assault tank! Although the AAT has missile launchers and a laser cannon, Yoda uses the Force to triumph.

Yoda's Clone Wars minifigure is just as wise and powerful as his classic minifigure, but he has a different look. The Clone Wars version of the ancient Jedi Grand Master has a bigger green head-mold—now with printed eyes—and a new, unique torso. But Yoda still wields his green lightsaber as he leads the clone army into battle against Separatist forces.

Yoda's head is made from rubber, like the Plo Koon (p.16), Kit Fisto, (p.27) and classic Yoda (p.8) minifigures

Two Yodas

This Clone Wars Yoda has been designed to look more cartoon-like than the classic Yoda minifigure (p. 8) to reflect the animated *Clone Wars* series. He has a bigger head, different ears, and large, painted eyes.

Yoda's head-mold has larger ears than the classic Yoda minifigure

Unique torso is printed with Yoda's simple tan robes and brown undershirt

Yoda might be small, but he is a lightsaber expert!

Yoda has short, unposeable leg pieces

Yoda

CLONE WARS JEDI LEADER

DATA FILE

SET: 7964 Republic Frigate
YEAR: 2011
PIECES: 3
EQUIPMENT: Lightsaber
VARIANTS: 1

During the Clone Wars, Anakin Skywalker becomes known throughout the LEGO *Star Wars* galaxy as the "Hero With No Fear." His minifigure battles for the Republic in eight LEGO sets, but could the exhausted, drawn expression on Anakin's unique face hint at the growing darkness within the brave Jedi Knight?

Dathomir Speeder (set 7957)
This 2011 LEGO set is the latest to feature the Clone Wars version of Anakin Skywalker. Asajj Ventress and her new Sith apprentice Savage Oppress attempt to take flight in their Dathomir speeder, but Anakin has other ideas!

Anakin Skywalker
CLONE WARS JEDI

Tousled reddish-brown hair is also seen on Mon Mothma's minifigure

Anakin's face has become battle-scarred during the Clone Wars

Anakin's Jedi robes have a more cartoon-like pattern than those seen on his classic Jedi Knight minifigure (p.28)

Clone Wars Anakin carries a blue lightsaber

DATA FILE
SET: 7957 Dathomir Speeder
YEAR: 2011
PIECES: 4
EQUIPMENT: Lightsaber
VARIANTS: 1

Battle for Geonosis (set 7869)

In this set, Luminara arrives on her BARC speeder to face a Separatist proton canon. There is nowhere for Luminara to store her lightsaber in the speeder, but she is very resourceful.

Luminara Unduli is a skilled and disciplined Jedi Master. This Clone Wars version of her minifigure has a double-sided head and wears more detailed Jedi robes than her classic minifigure. Clone Wars Luminara comes in just one set wearing all unique pieces apart from her headdress.

Non light-up lightsaber

Luminara's head piece is unique to this minifigure. It is more detailed than her 2005 classic version

No cape
This Clone Wars version of Luminara's minifigure appears without her cape. The headdress piece on this minifigure is the same as on the classic version of this dedicated Jedi Master.

Highly detailed torso with unique printing of Luminara's Jedi robes with colorful Mirialan symbol

Ornate Mirialan sash

Goggles on
The other side of Luminara's head piece shows her wearing goggles to keep out sand during sandstorms.

DATA FILE
SET: 7869 Battle for Geonosis
YEAR: 2011
PIECES: 4
EQUIPMENT: Lightsaber
VARIANTS: 1

Luminara Unduli
CLONE WARS JEDI MASTER

Plo Koon is a Kel Dor from the planet Dorin. He is a Jedi Master during the Clone Wars and a highly skilled pilot. His minifigure has a unique torso showing his Jedi robes and a unique head piece that displays both his Kel Dor origins and the antiox mask he wears so he can breathe when not on Dorin.

Republic Attack Gunship (set 7676)
In this 2008 set, the Republic's clone army has boarded a huge gunship to take on the Separatists in the harshest battlefields. Plo Koon rides a small speeder bike that can be deployed from the back of the heavily armored gunship.

Dark orange and dark bluish-gray rubber head-mold

Blade change
Plo Koon made his debut in 2008 in the Republic Gunship (set 7676). The set's box artwork originally showed Plo Koon with a green lightsaber, but this was changed to blue before its final release.

Plo Koon wears a fanged antiox breathing mask and he is rarely seen without his protective goggles

Blue-bladed lightsaber with silver hilt

Plo Koon
JEDI PILOT

Dark brown Jedi robe with white undershirt. The robe printing continues on the back of the torso

DATA FILE
SET: 8093 Plo Koon's Jedi Starfighter
YEAR: 2010
PIECES: 3
EQUIPMENT: Lightsaber
VARIANTS: 1

Jedi robes
The Jedi robes and belt that are printed on Nahdar's unique torso continue on the reverse, too.

Nahdar Vebb is a Mon Calamari Jedi Knight who trained under Jedi Master Kit Fisto. His minifigure only appears in one LEGO set, where he attacks General Grievous on his starfighter. Nahdar is sometimes impatient, but he is always passionate about protecting the LEGO *Star Wars* galaxy.

Bulging yellow eyes on either side of head have a wide field of vision

Mon Calamari
Nahdar's squid-like head is not unique: The solid plastic Mon Calamari head-mold is also used for the Admiral Ackbar and Mon Calamari officer minifigures.

Mon Calamari can breathe underwater for up to 30 hours

Nahdar wears Jedi robes in the traditional style, which include a tan tunic, white undershirt, and brown belt

Although young, Nahdar is skilled with a lightsaber. He can defeat four MagnaGuards on his own!

Nahdar Vebb
MON CALAMARI JEDI

DATA FILE
SET: 8095 General Grievous' Starfighter
YEAR: 2010
PIECES: 3
EQUIPMENT: Lightsaber
VARIANTS: 1

Wise Mace Windu is a Jedi General during the Clone Wars. His minifigure wields the same purple lightsaber as the classic Mace minifigure (p.9), but he now wears a tan Jedi tunic with no cape, and has new printed detail on his head piece. Mace fights for the Republic in three Clone Wars sets.

Republic Attack Shuttle (set 8019)

Mace Windu leads clone troopers into battle aboard this huge Republic attack shuttle. The Jedi General has his own LEGO seat inside the ship, which also has flick-fire missiles and deadly bombs to deploy!

Mace Windu
CLONE WARS JEDI GENERAL

Mace is one of the top lightsaber duelists in the galaxy

Mace's Clone Wars head piece is printed with a lot of detail, including brown eyes and a determined expression

Unique torso printed with tan tunic and white undershirt

Utility belt has a loop that Mace uses to hold his lightsaber

DATA FILE

SET: 7868 Mace Windu's Jedi Starfighter
YEAR: 2011
PIECES: 3
EQUIPMENT: Lightsaber
VARIANTS: 1

Republic Attack Gunship (set 7676)

Obi-Wan Kenobi tackles his bitter enemy Asajj Ventress in this 2008 set, which was the first to feature the Clone Wars version of Obi-Wan's minifigure. Jedi Plo Koon provides back-up.

Obi-Wan Kenobi is a public symbol of hope during the Clone Wars. Although his minifigure carries a lightsaber, Obi-Wan is known throughout the galaxy as "The Negotiator" because of his diplomacy skills and reluctance to use the powerful weapon in combat. Clone Wars Obi-Wan's calm demeanor has been tested in two sets since 2008.

This dark orange combed-over hair piece is only seen on Obi-Wan's Clone Wars minifigure

Obi-Wan's unique head piece has big, cartoon-like eyes and a dark orange beard

Different strokes

Obi-Wan has a different lightsaber in Pirate Tank (set 7753): Its hilt is light bluish-gray instead of metallic silver.

Traditional Jedi utility belt with a metallic clasp

Obi-Wan prefers to use his lightsaber to defend, not attack

Loose-fitting Jedi pants

Obi-Wan Kenobi
CLONE WARS NEGOTIATOR

DATA FILE

SET: 7753 Pirate Tank
YEAR: 2009
PIECES: 4
EQUIPMENT: Lightsaber
VARIANTS: 1

Jedi Council member Eeth Koth is an Iridonian Zabrak. His minifigure wears traditional Jedi robes and wields a green lightsaber. A specially designed head attachment features Eeth's short Zabrak horns and long, dark hair. He appears in just one LEGO set, aboard a Republic Frigate (set 7964).

DATA FILE

SET: 7964 Republic Frigate
YEAR: 2011
PIECES: 4
EQUIPMENT: Lightsaber
VARIANTS: 1

Eeth Koth
ZABRAK JEDI MASTER

Horned head and hair piece is made of rubber, not the usual ABS plastic

Unique face printing shows Eeth's simple tattoos

Eeth's hair is tied with traditional Iridonian rope. Two bunches hang over the front of Eeth's torso and a third hangs down the back

Torso is printed with a set of Jedi robes unique to Eeth

Eeth uses his strong connection to the Force to enhance his lightsaber skills

Zabrak horns
There are four Zabrak minifigures and their horned heads are all different. Darth Maul and Savage Opress share a head attachment but have different printing, Eeth's rubber head piece is unique, and Sugi's horns are printed on her standard LEGO head.

Aayla prefers using her lightsaber for defense rather than attack

Unique head top clips onto Aayla's standard LEGO head to attach her brown helmet and blue Twi'lek tentacles

Aayla Secura is a Twi'lek Jedi Knight. Her blue-skinned minifigure wears a brown Jedi costume and wields a blue lightsaber. Aayla only appears in one LEGO set, Clone Turbo Tank (set 8098), where she, Anakin, and Ahsoka lead their clone troopers against the ruthless bounty hunter Cad Bane.

Twi'lek skin can be almost any color, but Aayla's blue skin tone is distinctive even among Twi'leks

Aayla's unique torso is printed with her Jedi costume: a cropped brown top with just one sleeve

Standard LEGO lightsaber hilt

Aayla Secura
BLUE-SKINNED JEDI

Reverse Twi'lek
Aayla's tentacles hang down behind her minifigure's back. The back of her torso is printed with her Jedi clothes.

DATA FILE
SET: 8098 Clone Turbo Tank
YEAR: 2009
PIECES: 4
EQUIPMENT: Lightsaber
VARIANTS: 1

Jedi Shaak Ti is a powerful Clone Wars general. She also trains new clone cadets. Shaak is renowned for her skill and intellect, even though she only appears in one LEGO set. Her minifigure has red Togruta skin and a unique detachable piece with blue and white head-tails that clips onto her head.

DATA FILE
SET: 7931 T-6 Jedi Shuttle
YEAR: 2011
PIECES: 5
EQUIPMENT: Lightsaber, cape
VARIANTS: 1

Hollow horns on top of Shaak's head are called montrals

Unique red head piece printed with white Togruta markings

Shaak Ti only fights with her lightsaber when all other options have been exhausted

Shaak Ti wears a traditional Togruta akul-tooth headdress

Unique torso printed with Shaak's brown Jedi robes and belt

Shaak Ti
JEDI GENERAL

Head-tails
This unique piece was specially made for Shaak Ti. She has two head-tails at the front and one at the back. Shaak is an adult so her head-tails are fully-grown, unlike Ahsoka's (p.12).

The only other LEGO *Star Wars* minifigure with red hands is the Royal Guard

Ki-Adi-Mundi's large binary brain makes him extremely logical and a skilled tactician. He has a second heart just to support his brain

Unique head piece shows Ki-Adi-Mundi's white mustache and beard, and his pale Cerean eyes

Ki-Adi-Mundi is a Jedi from the planet Cerea. Highly intelligent, his minifigure is a member of the Jedi Council and a top Jedi General. Ki-Adi-Mundi has a specially designed additional head piece to house his extremely large Cerean brain. His minifigure flies into battle over the planet Geonosis in just one 2011 Clone Wars set.

Cerean head
Ki-Adi-Mundi's Cerean head is topped with a white ponytail. His binary brain piece has creases down the back, which are continued as printed lines on his head piece.

Unique torso is printed with Ki-Adi-Mundi's Jedi robes. His long vest is styled after ancient Cerean clothing

Utility belt has a clip to hold lightsaber

Ki-Adi-Mundi favors a defensive form of lightsaber combat

Ki-Adi-Mundi
JEDI TACTICIAN

DATA FILE
SET: 7959 Geonosian Starfighter
YEAR: 2011
PIECES: 4
EQUIPMENT: Lightsaber
VARIANTS: 1

Telepathic Jedi Saesee Tiin is a celebrated pilot in the Republic fleet. He is from the planet Iktotch and his minifigure has a unique piece with down-turned horns that fits onto his head piece. Saesee is an integral member of the Jedi Council, as well as a brave soldier. He wears his Jedi robes and wields his lightsaber with pride.

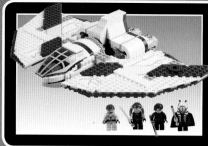

T-6 Jedi Shuttle (set 7931)

Saesee Tiin is exclusive to this LEGO set. He and three other Jedi travel to a distant battlefield on the Jedi shuttle. The shuttle is armed with flick missiles, and the cockpit can become an escape pod —should trouble arise.

Saesee Tiin
JEDI WARRIOR

Saesee's skin is very tough—able to withstand the strong winds of his home planet

Saesee's serious face can make him look quite intimidating sometimes!

Unique torso is printed with brown Jedi robes and a utility belt

Saesee's telepathic skills help during a lightsaber duel

Iktotchi skin

Saesee Tiin's telepathic powers have transformed the skin on his head, resulting in symmetrical markings.

DATA FILE

SET: 7931 T-6 Jedi Shuttle
YEAR: 2011
PIECES: 4
EQUIPMENT: Lightsaber
VARIANTS: 1

Unisex hair piece
Quinlan's hair is unique to his minifigure in LEGO *Star Wars*. However, the same piece is used for female minifigures in other LEGO themes, including LEGO Harry Potter, where it adorns the heads of Hermione Granger and Molly Weasley.

DATA FILE
SET: 7964 Republic Frigate
YEAR: 2011
PIECES: 4
EQUIPMENT: Lightsaber
VARIANTS: 1

Quinlan Vos is an unconventional Jedi. He is an expert Force tracker, able to locate anybody by following their trail—but he has also teetered on the edge of the dark side. His unkempt minifigure has messy hair, a stubbled face, and wears a rusty chestplate over his Jedi tunic. He spends much time undercover, which may be why he appears only in one LEGO set.

Quinlan sometimes uses a lightsaber fighting style that taps into dark side energies

Printed hair braid

Quinlan uses the Force to read the "memories" of inanimate objects

Quinlan paints a yellow stripe across his face to help with camouflage while he is tracking someone

Quinlan's blaster-proof chestplate is part of his Jedi uniform because he finds himself in danger more often than most

Utility belt conceals Quinlan's Jedi items when undercover

Quinlan Vos
JEDI TRACKER

Torso printing
The unique printing on Quinlan's torso continues on the reverse, depicting the back of his tunic and armor.

Obi-Wan Kenobi is now a Jedi Master and he has achieved much military success as a General during the Clone Wars. His minifigure has appeared in four LEGO *Star Wars* sets, as a slightly different variant in each one. In Ultimate Lightsaber Duel (7257), Obi-Wan wields a light-up lightsaber when forced to fight his former apprentice, Anakin Skywalker.

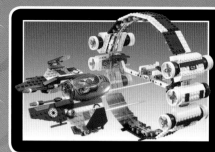

Jedi Starfighter with Hyperdrive Booster Ring (set 7661)
Obi-Wan Kenobi and his Jedi starfighter zip into hyperspace with the help of a hyperdrive booster ring in this 2007 set. It is the only set to features the latest variant of the minifigure.

Obi-Wan Kenobi wears a gold headset when piloting his Jedi Starfighter

Obi-Wan Kenobi
JEDI MASTER

STAR VARIANT

Light-up Jedi
A Light-up Lightsaber variant of Jedi Master Obi-Wan Kenobi appears in Ultimate Lightsaber Duel (set 7257). The variant is not wearing a pilot headset.

Cloaked Kenobi
Jedi Master Obi-Wan wears a Jedi cloak in two LEGO sets: General Grievous Chase (set 7255) and Ultimate Lightsaber Duel (set 7257). The Light-up Lightsaber variant in Ultimate Lightsaber Duel also wears a Jedi hood.

Obi-Wan is now a Jedi Master, but he still wears simple and practical Jedi robes

DATA FILE
SET: 7661 Jedi Starfighter with Hyperdrive Booster Ring
YEAR: 2007
PIECES: 4
EQUIPMENT: Lightsaber
VARIANTS: 4

This Obi-Wan variant has tan legs, but all three earlier variants of the minifigure have dark orange leg pieces

Jedi Starfighter with Hyperdrive Booster Ring (set 7661)

Jedi Master Kit Fisto first appears in this set. He provides backup for Obi-Wan Kenobi, although there is no place for him aboard the starfighter—unless he pilots it instead of Obi-Wan!

Kit Fisto is a green-skinned Jedi Master. His minifigure dresses in brown and gray Jedi robes and carries a green lightsaber. The long tentacles that grow from his head can sense emotions in the people around him. As a respected Jedi General, Kit fights alongside other Jedi Knights and leads troops into battle in two LEGO sets.

Head of rubber

Kit Fisto is one of three LEGO *Star Wars* minifigures to feature a head made from rubber instead of ABS plastic. The others are Yoda (p.8 and p.13) and Plo Koon (p.16). Rubber is easier to cast and can capture more detail, but it is prone to disintegrate.

Kit is a Nautolan. He has green skin, big, black eyes, and head tentacles

Unique torso with brown-and-gray Jedi robes and silver belt

Silver lightsaber hilt. The 2007 variant has a matte gray lightsaber hilt

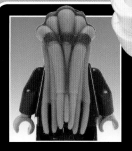

Tentacles

The back of Kit Fisto's specially designed head sculpt displays more of his sensory head tentacles.

Kit uses his ability to sense emotions to gain an advantage in battle: He can tell who is scared!

DATA FILE

SET: 8088 ARC-170 Starfighter
YEAR: 2010
PIECES: 3
EQUIPMENT: Lightsaber
VARIANTS: 1

Kit Fisto
JEDI GENERAL

Anakin Skywalker is now a lauded Jedi Knight. The minifigure has a battle-scarred face and a cyborg hand after Anakin faced many trials during the Clone Wars, but he has proven himself to be a hero of the LEGO *Star Wars* galaxy. Two variants of Anakin appear in three 2005 LEGO sets, one with a light-up lightsaber.

STAR VARIANT

Light-less
This non-Light-up Lightsaber Anakin was released in two LEGO sets: Jedi Starfighter and Vulture Droid (set 7256) and Ultimate Space Battle (set 7283). The variant wears a headset and no cape.

Anakin is the only LEGO minifigure to wear this hair piece in a dark flesh color

Anakin's unique LEGO head has a button to control his light-up lightsaber

Cyborg hand concealed by a black glove. Count Dooku cut off Anakin's hand

Facial scars are from a duel with Asajj Ventress during the Clone Wars

Dark Jedi tunic with black surcoat—this torso piece is exclusive to Anakin's Jedi Knight minifigure

Hip piece is integrated into the torso piece on Light-up Lightsaber minifigures

Anakin Skywalker
JEDI KNIGHT

The hilt of Anakin's blue light-up lightsaber is joined to his arm piece so electric current can flow through it from a battery in his torso

DATA FILE

SET: 7257 Ultimate Lightsaber Duel
YEAR: 2005
PIECES: 2
EQUIPMENT: Cape, lightsaber
VARIANTS: 2

Republic Swamp Speeder (set 8091)

Barriss is ready to take on the Separatists in her armored swamp speeder, which "hovers" above the ground thanks to hidden LEGO wheels. Barriss's minifigure is exclusive to this set.

Young Barriss Offee learns all she can from her experienced Jedi mentor, Luminara Unduli. Barriss wears her own Mirialan robes instead of regular Jedi attire, and she has a unique face, with blue lips and tattoos. Barriss appears in just one LEGO set, in which she wields a blue lightsaber.

DATA FILE

SET: 8091 Republic Swamp Speeder
YEAR: 2010
PIECES: 4
EQUIPMENT: Lightsaber, cape
VARIANTS: 1

Black version of brown Jedi hood

Mirialan tattoos are a sign of high achievement

Barriss is skilled in lightsaber combat

Mirialan skin tone

Barriss Offee and her Jedi Master, Luminara Unduli, are from the planet Mirial. To reflect their alien origins, their minifigures' heads and hands are differentiated by a distinctive skin color, which has a greenish hue.

Unique torso with black and blue stripes and belt pattern

Barriss Offee
LOYAL PADAWAN

Editors Hannah Dolan, Shari Last,
Victoria Taylor, and Matt Jones
Designers Anne Sharples and Jon Hall
Senior Producer Lloyd Robertson
Senior DTP Designer David McDonald
Managing Editor Simon Hugo
Design Manager Guy Harvey
Creative Manager Sarah Harland
Art Director Lisa Lanzarini
Publisher Julie Ferris
Publishing Director Simon Beecroft

Additional minifigures photographed by Huw Millington,
Ace Kim, Jeremy Beckett, and Tony Wood

First published in the United States in 2015
by DK Publishing
345 Hudson Street, New York, New York 10014

Contains material previously published in
LEGO® Star Wars® Character Encyclopedia (2011)

001-284485-Feb/15

Page design copyright ©2015 Dorling Kindersley Limited
A Penguin Random House Company

A catalog record for this book is available from
the Library of Congress.

ISBN: 978-5-0010-1295-5

Color reproduction by Media Development Printing Ltd, UK
Printed and bound in China

Dorling Kindersley would like to thank:
Jonathan W. Rinzler, Troy Alders, Rayne Roberts, Pablo
Hidalgo, and Leland Chee at Lucasfilm; Stephanie
Lawrence, Randi Sørensen, Lisbeth Langjkær, Jens
Kronvold Frederiksen, Chris Bonven Johansen, and John
McCormack at the LEGO Group; LEGO Star Wars
collectors Ace Kim and Huw Millington; Emma Grange,
Lisa Stock, Sarah Harland, Ellie Hallsworth, and Nicola
Brown for editorial support; and Owen Bennett for
design support on the cover.

www.dk.com
www.LEGO.com
www.starwars.com

A WORLD OF IDEAS:
SEE ALL THERE IS TO KNOW